25912

959.9 Walsh, John E.
WAL
        The Philippine
        Insurrection, 1899-
        1902

DATE			
SE 23 '81			
MY 25 '82			
DEC 1 6			
MAR 1 1989			
APR 1 2 1990			
NOV 2 9 1989			
FEB 2 1 1990			
APR 1 1 1990			
MAY 7 1990			
OCT 2 1 1992			

D1560810

© THE BAKER & TAYLOR CO

*The
Philippine
Insurrection*

THE PHILIPPINE INSURRECTION

When America emerged victorious from the Spanish-American War of 1898–9, many people of the Philippine Islands — who had been under the harsh rule of Spain for centuries — hoped for complete independence. But the United States, after bitter internal debate, decided to retain temporary possession of the islands. When they heard of this decision, a large force of Filipino rebels under the brilliant leadership of Emilio Aguinaldo, began an insurrection that was to continue for three years. The revolt ended only with the spectacular capture of Aguinaldo himself. Eventually, after achieving a stable government and a sound economy, the Philippines were given their independence by the United States.

PRINCIPALS

EMILIO AGUINALDO, thirty-year-old chief of the Filipino rebels. The insurrection centered around his legend and escapades and his rare abilities as a military and political strategist.

WILLIAM JENNINGS BRYAN, spokesman for those Americans who opposed annexation of the Philippines. As a candidate for president in 1900, he was defeated by William McKinley.

ADMIRAL GEORGE DEWEY, commander of the American fleet that smashed Spanish naval power in the Philippines. He accepted Aguinaldo's offer of a Filipino alliance against the Spanish ground troops that remained in the islands.

GENERAL FREDERICK FUNSTON, the thirty-six-year-old American army officer who conceived the daring plan for the capture of Aguinaldo, and who personally led the disguised raiding party on its dangerous mission.

GENERAL ARTHUR MACARTHUR, the American army commander whose troops routed Aguinaldo's forces in the first phase of the insurrection. He was the father of General Douglas Mac-Arthur of World War II fame.

PRESIDENT WILLIAM MCKINLEY, who wavered before advocating support of the Imperialists in their efforts to convince America that it had a mortal duty to annex and care for the Philippine Islands.

PRESIDENT THEODORE ROOSEVELT, who entered office after the assassination of McKinley in 1901. He continued America's enlightened policies in the islands.

LAZARO SEGOVIA and HILARIO PLACIDO, two Filipinos loyal to the United States, who posed as the officers in charge of General Funston's disguised raiding party. They accomplished the physical capture of Aguinaldo.

WILLIAM HOWARD TAFT, first civil governor of the Philippines; the man whose tact and understanding was responsible for the success of America's initial efforts to administer the islands.

Overleaf:
One of the greatest historic treasures of the Philippines is this photo-
graph. It shows General Emilio Aguinaldo being inaugurated as Presi-
dent of the first Philippine Republic at Malolos on January 23, 1899.

The Philippine Insurrection, 1899–1902

America's Only Try for an Overseas Empire

By John E. Walsh

FRANKLIN WATTS, INC.
NEW YORK/1973

*The authors and publisher of the Focus Books
wish to acknowledge the helpful editorial
suggestions of Professor Richard B. Morris.*

Photographs courtesy of:
Acme Photos: pp. 64 (top), 64 (bottom)
Charles Phelps Cushing: pp. xii, 14, 38, 42, 46, 58 (bottom)
Library of Congress: pp. 26, 60
New York Public Library: frontis, pp. 3, 10 (bottom),
    13, 17, 18, 21, 24, 28, 35, 36, 40, 45, 49, 53, 58 (top),
    62
Sawders-Cushing: pp. 8, 10 (top)

Library of Congress Cataloging in Publication Data

Walsh, John E.
    The Philippine insurrection, 1899–1902.

    (A Focus book)
    SUMMARY: Traces the causes, events, and results
of the insurrection resulting from the United States
decision not to grant Philippine independence at the
end of the Spanish-American war.
    Bibliography: p.
    1. Philippine Islands–History–Insurrection, 1899-
1901–Juvenile literature. [1. Philippine Islands–History
–Insurrection, 1899-1901]
I. Title.
D5679.W35   959.9'031   72-8817
ISBN 0-531-02462-8

Contents

The
Philippine
Insurrection

Prologue:
No Simple Answers

On a bright, hot morning in mid-May of 1898, a gleaming white steam launch chugged its way across the wide waters of Manila Bay, the principal harbor of the Philippine Islands and the scene of Admiral George Dewey's victory over the Spanish fleet just a few weeks before. In the group aboard the launch was a serious-faced young man whose dark eyes betrayed no sign of emotion. This was Emilio Aguinaldo, thirty-year-old leader of the Filipino rebels. At this moment his name was virtually unknown to Americans. All too soon it would become tragically familiar.

For three years Aguinaldo had commanded a large and dedicated force of *Insurrectos*, in their battle to rid the islands of the centuries-old domination of Spain. Ill-trained and always lacking in arms and supplies, the rebels had fought well, but with little success. Now, quite suddenly, a dramatic turn of events had given their long struggle new hope. America, the young giant of the New World, had also declared war on Spain.

In April 1898, America's deep interest in the social and political unrest in another Spanish territory — Cuba, which was only 90 miles from Florida — had finally brought Spain and America into a violent disagreement that involved both ground and naval forces. A portion of the Spanish fleet was then stationed in the Philippines, and a task force under Admiral George Dewey was quickly dispatched to the islands to do battle with this isolated flotilla.

On May 1, Dewey's ships steamed into Manila Bay and in a

A portrait of the famous Philippine insurrectionist leader Emilio Aguinaldo.

[1]

few short hours of fighting they completely smashed the Spanish naval force. The victory, whose echoes rang around the world, was a sensational one (unbelievably, there had been only one American casualty). As a result of this naval triumph, the Spanish ground troops in the Philippines were isolated. Dewey's ships quickly set up a blockade that would await the arrival of the American army to complete the occupation of the islands.

The people of the Philippines had enthusiastically hailed the American victory at Manila Bay. Aguinaldo and his rebels, their smoldering hopes of freedom suddenly ablaze again, were eager to join in the task of wiping out the last vestiges of Spanish rule. It was to offer Admiral Dewey a Filipino alliance with the United States that Aguinaldo had come to Manila.

The small launch drew alongside the battle cruiser *Olympia*, Dewey's flagship. Accompanied by his aides, Aguinaldo was piped on board and greeted by the admiral himself. The contrast in the appearance of the two men was striking, and interestingly symbolized the differences between their countries. Dewey, impressive in his uniform, was a tall, heavy, white-haired man, with a full, drooping mustache and a controlled manner. His background included the best military education and long command experience. Aguinaldo, like most of his fellow Filipinos, was short in stature and slight in build, soft-spoken and dignified in bearing. Although he had no real military training and little formal education, he was a man of exceptional cunning and courage, as well as a military and political strategist of intuitive brilliance. His many exploits in battle had already made him a legend. It was whispered by his fol-

Portrait of Dewey at Manila Bay. Actually a commodore during the famous battle and later made admiral, Dewey watches from the bridge of his flagship Olympia *as his squadron's big guns pound the Spanish Asiatic fleet.*

[2]

lowers that some mysterious power turned away all bullets and knives, keeping him safe even during the most violent fight.

For more than an hour Dewey and Aguinaldo conferred alone in the admiral's private quarters. (Unfortunately, no official records were kept of this meeting, a fact that would later lead to difficulty.) Aguinaldo then climbed back into the waiting launch and sped back to shore. He immediately began sending messages throughout the Philippines. The time had come at last, he proclaimed with joy, for a final offensive against the hated Spanish oppressors. Filipino patriots were now the allies of the American liberators.

At that time the Filipinos felt that it was a blessing to be allied with the United States. But in time, the alliance would prove to be a curse. After the defeat of the Spanish, a disagreement would arise over the question of immediate independence for the Philippines, and American policy would be decided in favor of holding onto their new possession, at least temporarily. Tragically, as a result of this decision, American and Filipino forces would clash in a bitter struggle, as bloody and devastating as anything that had occurred under the Spanish rule.

Eventually, American power and determination would triumph. But the story does not end there. After almost a half-century of American rule — a time of steadily growing prosperity as well as social and political advance — the Philippines in 1946 were at last given their independence, freely and fully, by the country that had earlier fought to possess them.

Looking back, it would be easy to say that America's Philippine adventure was nothing but a colossal mistake, paid for with the lives of 5,000 Americans and 20,000 Filipinos, with many thousands of people wounded, and millions of dollars wasted in military expenditure and destruction of property. Such a conclusion seems unavoidable to many people. But that is a judgment made many years after the fact, when the details of the Philippine Insurrection have largely been forgotten. To the men of the time, submerged in the flow of daily pressures, surrounded by old traditions and emerging opinions, the mistake was not so obvious.

Like most tragedies, this one was not seen in its full terror at the beginning. It only developed step by step. To follow those steps is to glimpse an often sad story, involving high aspirations as well as woeful error, brave deeds as well as brutality.

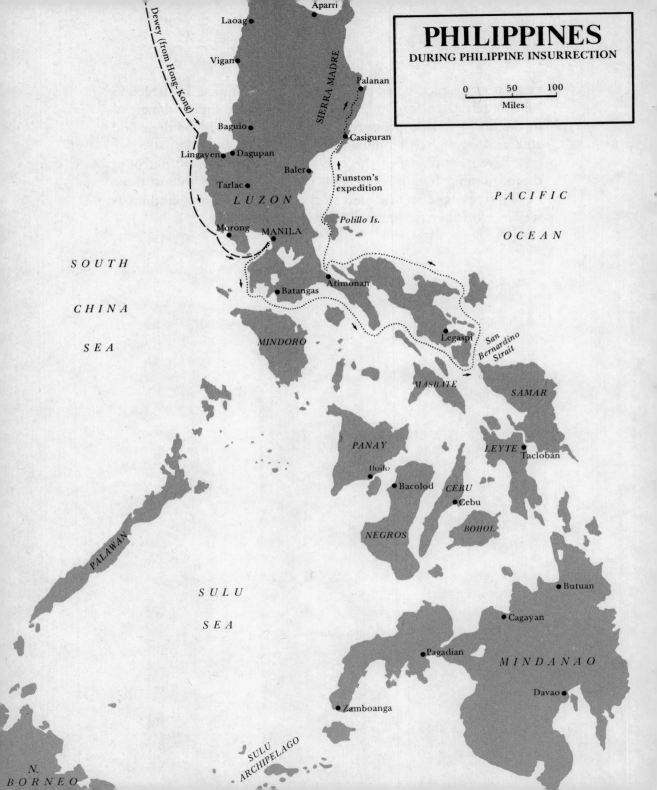

Dewey (from Hong-Kong)

Aparri

Laoag

Vigan

Palanan

SIERRA MADRE

Casiguran

Baguio

Lingayen • Dagupan

Baler

Tarlac •

Funston's expedition

LUZON

Polillo Is.

PACIFIC

Morong • MANILA

OCEAN

SOUTH

Batangas • Atimonan

CHINA

SEA

MINDORO

Legaspi

San Bernardino Strait

MASBATE

SAMAR

PANAY

LEYTE

Iloilo

Tacloban

Bacolod

CEBU

Cebu

BOHOL

NEGROS

PALAWAN

Butuan

SULU

Cagayan

SEA

MINDANAO

Pagadian

Davao

Zamboanga

N.

SULU

BORNEO

ARCHIPELAGO

PHILIPPINES
DURING PHILIPPINE INSURRECTION

0   50   100

Miles

The Philippine Islands

The Philippine Islands are a narrow archipelago, straggling for more than 1,000 miles through the China Sea between Japan to the north and western Australia to the south. This immense chain is comprised of no fewer than 7,000 separate islands, most of them small. Even today the greater number of them are unnamed and uninhabited. The Philippines' climate is tropical, with extremely hot, humid summers, during which the rain falls in torrents for days on end. It is a lush land, abundant in fertile soil and natural resources, including many minerals and spices.

First discovered by Ferdinand Magellan during his epic circumnavigation of the world in the sixteenth century, the islands soon came under the rule of Spain. Unfortunately, in succeeding centuries, the Spaniards proved autocratic and unsympathetic. Restrictive laws, heavy taxes, social barriers, and a lack of real educational opportunity reduced the natives to a state of virtual slavery. Religious missionaries from Spain — in charge of such things as schools, charities, tax collecting, public works — were surprisingly lacking in foresight, nor did they really understand the deprived condition of the population. In time, the church in the Philippines accumulated vast wealth, based mainly on its ownership of some half-million acres of the best land. While the people remained nominally Christian, the church and its administrators soon came to be regarded with intense dislike, even hatred.

By 1900, a native population of about 7 million people occupied perhaps a thousand of the islands, with the largest settlements concentrated on Luzon (about the size of Illinois) and Mindinao (about the size of Indiana). The blood that ran in Filipino veins, a mixture of many strains, was very ancient and its origins were difficult to trace. Generally, it is believed, four main

sources contributed: Malay, Chinese, Aborigine, and stock from such surrounding lands as Japan, Vietnam, and Indonesia. A number of individual groups, such as the Negritos and the Moros (Mohammedans), lived a life apart. The language of the islands had, during centuries of development, splintered into more than eighty dialects, most of them based on the Malay tongue. Tagalog, Visayan, and Bicol, with one or two others, were its main divisions.

Most Filipinos were independent farmers, living either on their own small plots of land or in villages that were isolated by the thick jungle foliage that surrounded them. Houses in these villages were little more than huts, usually raised on stilts, with ladders reaching up to the high doorways. There were no good roads and no highways. The dusty village streets, as well as the dirt roads that penetrated the wild country between towns, became ribbons of muck during the rainy season. Transportation was usually by ox cart or on horseback. The lone primitive railroad in the country ran from Manila to Lingayen Gulf, a distance of just over 100 miles. Except for a few cigar factories, industry was almost nonexistent.

Dotting the northern island landscape were a number of small, fairly modern cities, in which lived a total of perhaps a million people. But only one of these cities, Manila, could make any pretense to cultural or commercial importance. In Manila lived most of the Spanish officials and colonists, together with Philippine natives and people from all over Europe and the East. The most ancient part of Manila, known as the old city, was protected by an encircling stone wall of huge proportions: 30 feet high by 40 feet wide. Adjoining this was the new city, twice the size of the old, but with the same, almost medieval charm pervading its narrow streets and dark, shuttered houses. A busy, cosmopolitan center,

A typical Filipino farmer plowing rice fields using water buffalo.

[9]

Manila offered its 300,000 inhabitants a large number of theaters, restaurants, bars, a dozen small newspapers, arenas for bull-fighting and cock-fighting, as well as the varied merchandise that entered its thriving port from all over the world.

Ordinary Americans, however, at the beginning of 1898, were only dimly aware of the far-away Philippine Islands. To most of them, the name represented just a rather backward Spanish possession, located somewhere 8,000 miles across the Pacific. Only with the coming of the Spanish-American War, and Dewey's smashing victory at Manila Bay, did the islands become a part of the American consciousness.

Above: a Filipino village of thatched houses on the island of Luzon. Below: one of the principal business streets in Manila at the turn of the century.

Early Signs of
Trouble for America

Emilio Aguinaldo's call to arms spread through the islands like wildfire. The rebels quickly converged on Luzon, setting up makeshift camps, organizing, drilling, and consolidating supplies. Within a surprisingly short time Aguinaldo had under his immediate command a force of no less than 30,000 men, all of them impatient for action.

It was not long before they had that action. Only nine days after the first call — and while the Filipinos were still more or less disorganized — a small Spanish force ambushed a rebel ammunition train. After some fierce fighting, the attackers were driven off and the train saved, giving the Filipinos a heady taste of victory and inflaming their desire for a general attack. Thereafter they descended jubilantly on town after town in Luzon, forcing the Spanish into a gradual pull-back toward the safety of Manila.

With the blockade set up by the American ships, and with American troops on the way to join the Filipino thousands, the Spanish well knew they had no hope of a military victory. But in Manila, behind the stout walls of the old city, they hoped to withstand a siege. Some twist of fate, perhaps an armistice, might yet leave them in possession of a large enough slice of territory to give them some bargaining power.

By the middle of June 1898, the central Luzon plain had been

Luzon warriors of the Macabebe tribe. Small and very fierce, they were excellent fighters. Known among the Americans as "Little Macs," they had long hated Aguinaldo, and some of them accompanied General Funston on his famous expedition later in the insurrection.

[12]

cleared of Spanish forces and was under complete control of the Filipino rebels. Crowded within Manila were about 15,000 Spanish regulars in addition to the large civilian population. Aguinaldo now set his men to sealing the city, and in an amazingly short time the metropolis was ringed with 14 miles of siege trenches. The Filipinos then captured an outlying power station and cut off most of the city's water supply. For those people within the city, living conditions quickly deteriorated as food, water, and medical supplies dwindled.

Aguinaldo, feeling that under these conditions the Spanish must soon surrender, in a burst of enthusiasm issued a proclamation to his countrymen officially announcing the birth of the Philippine Republic. A flag was hurriedly designed and soon it could be seen flying over the trenches and from the masts of the half-dozen steam launches that made up the Filipino "navy."

To Admiral Dewey, the ranking American commander on the scene, Aguinaldo's impetuous action was not only premature but unfortunate. The whole Philippine situation had developed so rapidly that no final policy for it had been set by the United States. Whether the Filipinos were actually to be given their freedom, and allowed full control of the islands, was a matter of great uncertainty. Thus Dewey neither opposed Aguinaldo nor showed any sign of approval. The admiral simply kept quiet and waited.

Late in June the American reinforcements began to arrive by troopship. During the ensuing five weeks, as company after company of soldiers came ashore from their transports and arms and ammunition were piling up impressively at the docks, the watch-

A company of Igorrote spearmen drilling in Caloocan, later the scene of a pitched battle. Sketch was made by an American artist from his cell window after he had been captured by the insurgents.

[15]

ing Aguinaldo could not help wondering. Why were so many American troops needed? His own 30,000 men, who could be reinforced if necessary to twice that number, could easily overpower the Spanish in Manila. And thereafter, were not the islands to belong to the Filipinos? To Aguinaldo it seemed an appalling waste of effort to bring in such a huge American force where they were not needed.

Inevitably, Aguinaldo's suspicions became aroused — perhaps the American did *not* intend to confer independence! He had also become embittered over Dewey's cool response to his authority and to his impassioned Proclamation of Independence. So, in this mood of doubt and resentment, the rebel leader began a subtle campaign of disruption to make his presence felt.

To his rebel chiefs Aguinaldo gave orders that there was to be no cooperation with the Americans without his personal written permission. Manual labor, supplies of fresh food, camping areas, and even the island's primitive transportation were suddenly unavailable to the arriving American troops. The result was a constant flurry of official documents between the Filipino and American headquarters. Dewey, reporting these developments to Washington, confessed that "the most difficult problem will be how to deal with the insurgents under Aguinaldo, who has become aggressive and even threatening towards our army."

Another serious problem also threatened to erupt at this time, but was avoided by Dewey's prompt and forceful handling. The sudden release of the Philippines from Spanish control had aroused the interest of other European nations in the islands' future, both for their own valuable resources as well as their position as a trading focal point in the Orient. Germany especially had moved swiftly, sending a number of warships to that area of the Pacific.

American troops departing for Manila in 1898.

[16]

BE CAREFUL

Supposedly they were on the scene as "observers"; in reality the Germans were there to probe the possibility of adding the Philippines to Germany's other Pacific holdings. Dewey bore this naval intrusion with patience until the German commander began patrolling Manila Bay itself — not bothering to acknowledge the American presence and even holding private talks with Aguinaldo.

Finally, Dewey forced a showdown. He informed the German commander, Admiral Von Diederichs, that if the latter's interference did not cease immediately, there would be "war, here and now." Diederichs, who was under strict orders to avoid all conflict, assured the American admiral that his country had no designs on the Philippines, apologized for his harrassing tactics, and then took his ships away to "observe" from afar. While this incident, in the general scope of history, was a fairly minor one, it played an important part later: it helped to convince many Americans that a free Philippine Republic would be quickly gobbled up by one of the large European powers.

Contemporary cartoon shows Uncle Sam's displeasure at Germany's meddling in the Philippine situation in 1898.

The Surrender of
Spanish Manila

By August 1898, the Spanish forces in Manila had been suffering under siege for three long months. Both sides — the sealed-in Spanish and the Filipino insurgents in their trenches — had begun to feel the strain of a stalemate. Frequently shots were exchanged along with shouted insults and threats of future reprisal. But despite their hardship, the Spanish would not yield. Three times Aguinaldo, acting on his own, had called for surrender, and each time the Spanish had disdainfully refused.

This Spanish decision to hold Manila was dictated in part by military pride as well as a faint hope that the situation might turn in Spain's favor. Even so, the Spanish forces were still very afraid of what might happen if the rebel horde was allowed to enter the city. In the hearts of most Filipinos there was an undying hatred of their former rulers, and the Spanish had no doubt that surrender to Aguinaldo would bring widespread slaughter of themselves and wanton destruction of all Spanish property.

It was this fear, in fact, that helped resolve the situation. With food and water almost gone and sickness increasing daily, the Spanish realized that it was useless to attempt to hold out any longer. They therefore made a secret arrangement by which Manila could be given up directly to the Americans (who at this point had 10,000 troops ready for action). It was agreed by the Spanish defenders that a mock attack would be mounted from the American sector, with both sides doing much aimless and noisy

Old Spanish fortifications around Manila defended by obsolete artillery. Such defenses were useless against modern weapons of the day.

[20]

shooting, yet withholding the use of artillery. Dewey's ships would then blast away for a few minutes with naval gunfire at a disused portion of the old city, following which the American troops would advance against token opposition. Aguinaldo, who knew nothing of this clandestine plan, was told that he would have to hold his men outside the city when the action began. This unwelcome order angered and puzzled the Filipino leader, and he replied that he could not guarantee to restrain his excited forces.

The sham battle began on the morning of August 13, 1898. Within a few hours Manila was in American hands. To prevent Aguinaldo from advancing, troops swept through the streets and threw up a defense perimeter before the *Insurrectos*, who had indeed begun to infiltrate.

That very same day, by sheer coincidence, the Spanish forces in Cuba surrendered, and the Spanish-American War came to an end.

The Argument Over
Philippine Independence

With the American victory came the urgent problem of deciding what to do with the conquered Spanish territories — principally Cuba and the Philippines. The question with regard to the Philippines was especially difficult, for there was a large and outspoken portion of the American public that demanded the islands be kept under American control. This faction soon received the label "Imperialists." President William McKinley, although wavering before he advocated acquiring the islands, was a member of this faction. Opposing them were the "Anti-Imperialists," who insisted that the Philippines should be given full and immediate independence because America had no actual right to keep those islands. William Jennings Bryan, who had been defeated by McKinley for the presidency in 1900, was a member of this group. A third faction suggested combining both independence and American control — the islands to be completely self-governing with the United States enjoying a favored trade and economic position. In the Senate, the press, and throughout the country, the debate raged for months, while the American Peace Commission met with Spanish representatives in Paris to draw up a formal treaty.

Today it is difficult to recapture the confused atmosphere of conflicting opinion in which this Philippine debate was conducted. Each side tended to oversimplify its own position and to belittle that of its opponents. Bryan, for instance, speaking to a large audience in Chicago, declared that "when the desire to steal becomes uncontrollable in an individual he is declared to be a kleptomaniac and is sent to an asylum. When the desire to grab land becomes uncontrollable in a nation we are told 'the currents of destiny are flowing through the hearts of men'."

Many people agreed with this view. Conscious of the ideals upon which the United States itself had been founded, they denounced any attempt to deny full freedom to another country, particularly if military action was needed to impose American control. The highly respected historian Henry Adams pointedly expressed this attitude in a private letter. "I fully share the alarm and horror," he said, "of seeing poor weak McKinley plunge into an inevitable war to conquer the Philippines, contrary to every principle of our lives and history . . . I turn green in bed at midnight if I think of the horror of a year's war in the Philippines . . . We must slaughter a million or two of foolish Malays in order to give them the comforts of flannel petticoats and electric railways."

And yet the "destiny" of which the Imperialists spoke seemed very real at the time, particularly when it became clear that America could not simply abandon the islands to an uncertain fate. The liberation of a small, weak nation like the Philippines, the Imperialists insisted, carried responsibilities — it had been for just such high ideals that America had gone to war with Spain in the first place. Were the Philippine Islands, at this point in their history, capable of self-government? In the opinion of many observers, it did not seem that they were. Constant unrest and internal strife, they insisted, would be the most likely outcome of premature Philippine independence. Moreover, what was to prevent some other large nation, less bothered than America by ethical questions, from taking over the unprotected islands — Germany, for instance? (Eventually, in fact, Spain did sell her other Pacific territories to Germany.) And who could say that Spain herself might not try to repossess the islands? If that did happen, would the United States be bound to come a second time to their assistance?

The Imperialist camp, on the other hand, made no secret of

President William McKinley.

[25]

William Jennings Bryan in a typical pose while addressing a large audience.

its conviction that the Philippines were necessary to the growing American economic empire. Already annexed by the United States were such Pacific outposts as Wake, Midway, and the Hawaii group. Combined with the Philippines, these could be the first stepping stones to the lucrative markets of Asia. It was Senator Albert Beveridge who, in a speech on the Senate floor, best summed up this attitude. The power that ruled the Pacific in the twentieth century, he ringingly declared, was the power that would rule the world. "And," he added, "with the Philippines, that power is and will forever be, the American Republic."

Furthermore, it was said — with a good deal of truth — that a large portion of the Philippine population itself was definitely in favor of annexation because the Filipinos realized that the power of the United States was vital to their future. The Anti-Imperialists loudly replied that this was not so, and that most Filipinos were against annexation. The question at the moment was beyond practical settlement, but it was true, at any rate, that all of the leaders of the rebel faction were urgently calling for independence.

The protectorate status suggested by a few — which would allow the Filipinos to govern themselves but with the advice and protection of the United States — was ruled out by most people as being highly impractical. Such an arrangement would involve heavy costs and no return; there might be confrontations with other nations drawn by the promise of large commercial rewards. Moreover, it would impose on the United States an unwanted and uncertain military burden.

Aguinaldo Threatens to Fight

While this historic argument was occupying America, Aquinaldo and his lieutenants watched and listened apprehensively. When the peace treaty with Spain provided that the Philippines be ceded to the United States (in return for a payment of $20 million), Aguinaldo understandably became alarmed.

Now almost convinced that America intended to keep the islands permanently, Aguinaldo began issuing impassioned denunciations of the "immoral" actions of the United States and demanding prompt recognition of a Filipino government. Finally, in his capacity as president of the Revolutionary Council, he bluntly stated that war would follow any attempt to take permanent possession of his homeland. "My nation cannot remain indifferent," he announced, "in view of such a violent and aggressive seizure . . . my government is disposed to open hostilities." Unfortunately, few Americans were inclined to believe that Aguinaldo meant what he said.

In the United States, in fact, Aguinaldo's threatening manifesto was looked upon merely as a bothersome item in the continuing debate. But in Manila it was a different matter, for here American and Filipino were face to face across the neutral zone that circled the city. Taunts, insults, and obscenities were constantly hurled back and forth, and at night in Manila's narrow streets, attacks on Americans by angered Filipino civilians using the murderous bolo knife, became common. United States soldiers quickly learned to travel in pairs and to carry loaded weapons.

Emilio Aguinaldo (center, seated), chief of the insurgent Filipinos, and a group of his followers.

[29]

Through the month of January 1899, Aguinaldo and the revolutionary government continued to seek reassurance from the Americans. They asked that no more troops be sent, that no more territory be occupied, and that some interim concessions be made in the direction of self-government. But the American military command in the Philippines had no power to grant any of these requests.

Consumed with worry and frustration, on January 20 the Filipino Revolutionary Cabinet voted full power to Aguinaldo to begin hostilities at his own discretion. He was given full command of not only the 30,000 men around Manila, but also of the additional thousands scattered throughout Luzon and the provinces. An estimate placed their total number at about 80,000; the Americans had just over 20,000, only some of whom were in Manila, and of those in the city not all were available for combat. If war came, the Americans would be outnumbered by at least five to one.

Aguinaldo's strategy for a general offensive had already been drawn up. It was to begin with a surprise attack on the Manila barracks, initiated by disguised infiltrators. Then a massive push by the insurgents outside the city was to be joined by Filipino sympathizers already inside. Attackers in the city who did not have arms, Aguinaldo directed, "should not attempt to secure rifles from their dead enemies, but shall pursue slashing right and left with bolos." On the housetops along the streets where the American troops would pass, he said, there should be placed in readiness: "stones, timbers, red-hot iron, heavy furniture, as well as boiling water, oil, molasses, rags soaked in coal oil ready to be lighted and thrown down." With the numerical odds against them, and facing such a fiercely dedicated enemy, the Americans' position — even granting the superior training and equipment of United States troops — was by no means impregnable.

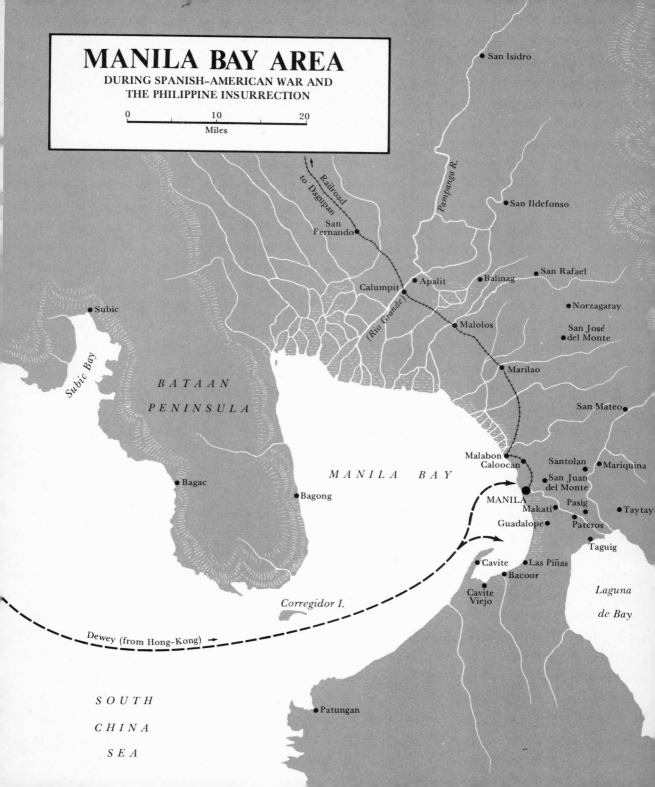

MANILA BAY AREA
DURING SPANISH-AMERICAN WAR AND
THE PHILIPPINE INSURRECTION

0   10   20
Miles

• San Isidro

Railroad to Dagupan

Pampanga R.

• San Ildefonso

San Fernando •

Calumpit • Apalit
• Balinag   • San Rafael

(Rio Grande)
• Malolos
• Norzagaray

• San José del Monte

• Subic

Subic Bay

• Marilao

BATAAN PENINSULA

• San Mateo

• Bagac

MANILA BAY

Malabon •
Caloocan
• Santolan   • Mariquina

San Juan del Monte

• Bagong

MANILA
Makati •   • Pasig
• Taytay

Guadalope •
Pateros

• Taguig

Cavite •   • Las Piñas

Corregidor I.
• Bacoor

Cavite Viejo

Laguna

de Bay

Dewey (from Hong-Kong) →

SOUTH

CHINA

SEA

• Patungan

At this point, with the United States Senate still trying to reach an acceptable answer to the Philippine dilemma, quite suddenly and unexpectedly on the night of February 4, 1899, fighting broke out.

The Insurrection Begins

No one has yet solved the riddle as to just who ignited the spark of the insurrection. Aguinaldo later claimed it was set off by the Americans on orders from Washington in hopes of influencing the Senate deliberations — to make it appear that the Filipinos were unstable and untrustworthy. This was denied, and Aguinaldo himself was accused of being the instigator, also with the hope of influencing American public opinion. It was further said that the rebel leader wanted to show that, against all expectations, the ragged insurgents would not be afraid to attack the American regulars.

If it *was* Aguinaldo who began the war, then it was a fatal mistake on his part. Although he was, like his followers, a courageous man, he had miscalculated the mood of the American people, most of whom would never back down in the face of an attack. No one in America wanted another war, especially since one had just been concluded, but neither did anyone seriously believe that a conflict in the Philippines could last for more than a few weeks.

Perhaps the insurgents had no more in mind than harrassment, perhaps they had some hope of creating temporary chaos and consternation. If so, the plan very quickly got out of hand. The flare-up — at the small jungle outpost of San Juan del Monte — started a blaze that in a matter of hours spread along both fronts. Aguinaldo wasted no time in declaring that a state of war existed. He immediately ordered a general attack on Manila.

Rebel artillery was brought into play, and twice the insurrectionists attempted a charge. They were easily thrown back, retreating in amazement at the Americans' vastly superior firepower and marksmanship. Throughout that first night there was much blind firing into the darkness, with occasional light forays by the Filipinos. Then, with the coming of dawn, fighting subsided. Over the centuries, it had become Philippine custom only to do battle in the coolness of night, avoiding the terrific heat of the day. Even the Spanish had fallen into this habit, so Aguinaldo's men were totally unprepared for what happened next.

Less than three hours after the rebels had withdrawn to their own lines, American heavy guns opened up on them. This fire came from United States army artillery in Manila and ships in the harbor (brand new telescopic sights gave astonishing accuracy to Dewey's 500-pound shells). The bombardment was followed by a completely unlooked-for American assault. Half of the combat troops in the city, about 5,000 men, under the command of General Arthur MacArther, swept across the river directly at Aguinaldo's center, stormed the hills opposite, and entirely routed the astounded Filipino rebels.

By noon of February 5, Aguinaldo's shocked forces had retreated to the cover of the Luzon jungles, where they expected to gain time for reorganizing a defense on more familiar terrain. But the other half of the American force had by this time moved out of the city to join the battle, and by evening Aguinaldo's thousands were again on the run. Americans pursued them for two miles through the dense jungle until recall was sounded.

The American victory was overwhelming and the battle figures reflected the uselessness of further resistance. The Americans had suffered fewer than 250 casualties, of whom only 50 had been killed. Among the Filipinos, there were more than 4,000 casualties, of whom nearly 1,000 men had died.

Filipino insurgents stage an evening attack on an American barracks in Manila, from a drawing by an American artist present at the time.

[34]

To the American public, this fresh outbreak of fighting was nearly unbelievable. How could it have happened while the debate over the future of the Philippines was in progress? The American reaction was angry, even furious. Aguinaldo's attack, it was said, was "insane," and the Filipinos were "babes of the jungle." A bitter editorial in the *New York Times* said that: "The Filipinos have chosen a bloody way to demonstrate their incapacity for self-government." American dignity had been insulted, American assistance had been repaid by ingratitude, and many Americans demanded that those who would attack their nation unprovoked be "thoroughly thrashed."

Across the United States, debate and argument rose to new heights of excitement, as newspaper headlines fed the turmoil. It was in this atmosphere of amazed resentment, wounded pride, and martial spirit, that the United States Senate convened to vote on the peace treaty with Spain. The treaty was ratified on February 6, 1899, and a week later the Senate declared that the Philippine Islands were annexed to the United States — though not permanently. At some unspecified time in the future, when the Filipinos had shown themselves ready for self-government, and when the country was pacified and economically strong, the Philippines would be granted their full independence. Thus the entire controversy had, in effect, come down to compromise: America was to keep the Philippines, but not forever. The people of the islands could look forward to their day of freedom.

Not surprisingly, this arrangement was hailed by a large portion of the Philippine population as the most desirable one possible — a few years of American aid, protection and instruction,

General Arthur MacArthur, whose troops routed Aguinaldo's men around Manila. He was the father of General Douglas MacArthur of World War II fame.

then independence. For Aguinaldo and the other rebel leaders, however, this promise of future freedom was not sufficient; nor did the superiority of the American forces serve to intimidate them. While they must have known it was hopeless, they chose to continue the fight.

In open warfare, even against great odds, the disciplined, well-trained, and well-supplied American army could not be beaten. Although it had to deal with the constant, oppressive heat (in one early action, for example, twenty-five men fell from heat prostration alone), the flooding rains that turned the ground to an ocean of mud, disrupting lines and tactics, as well as the impossible jungle growth that impeded maneuvers, the Americans still had little difficulty routing the rebels.

During the first half of the year 1899, town after town on Luzon fell easily to the American advance, as the rebels retreated deeper and deeper into the interior. The names of these towns became very familiar to the American public as it followed the progress of their troops: Caloocan, Pasig, Malolos, Calumpit, Balinag, San Isidro. Sometimes the rebels fought hard before yielding, but usually resistance simply melted away. When the battle-ready Americans drew up before Iloilo, for instance, they found that the place was already in friendly hands, for the navy had put a company of marines ashore a few hours previously and the town had been taken almost without a shot.

By late summer of 1899 it seemed only a matter of days until the Filipino insurrection would be smashed beyond hope. In this desperate situation, Aguinaldo requested a cease-fire of three months, so that he might discuss with his cabinet the terms they

Artist's sketch of the battle action before Caloocan on February 10, 1899. General MacArthur's Pennsylvania Volunteers are behind the wall in front of the church.

[39]

were to ask for surrender. Major General Ewell Otis, the new American commander, replied that he had no power to offer terms of any kind, that full and immediate surrender was the only course open to the rebels. To this, Aguinaldo offered no response, but the fighting did die down and it began to appear that America's Philippine adventure was nearing a conclusion.

Above, a Utah battery in action at Caloocan. Below, an American commander makes an inspection of the suburbs of Malolos shortly after the fall of the town.

Guerrilla tactics of the insurgents included wrecking American supply trains. Sketch shows them being driven off by U.S. scouts.

The Second Phase—
Guerrilla Warfare

While all this fighting was going on, United States policy toward the new acquisition was crystallizing. A government commission was sent to study all aspects of the country's needs, and its report was thorough. The commission said there should be a large degree of self-government in local matters, with as many posts as possible being filled by the Filipinos themselves. Radical reforms must be instituted in such fields as education, agriculture, civil service, and tax collection. Corruption of all kinds, which had become almost a way of life in the islands, was to be ruthlessly suppressed.

Announcement of these aims brought further support for United States policy; in fact, even many of those who had originally opposed annexation were now glad to cooperate. But Aguinaldo and his men still refused to relinquish their dream, so they fixed their hopes on the presidential elections that were to take place in the United States in November 1900. It was not impossible, they felt, that a new party would be brought into office, and that the Anti-Imperialist's opinion would at length prevail. If this did happen, freedom for the Philippines might still be achieved. Meanwhile, it was necessary to keep the issue alive, and since the rebels had no chance against the American army in open combat, the only alternative was a guerrilla campaign.

The heavily-wooded and vegetation-choked terrain of the Philippines was perfectly suited to guerrilla warfare. It allowed small bands of men to strike suddenly at weak points and unprotected areas of the American lines. These men could then mount hit-and-run maneuvers against the towns, engage in ambuscades and small patrol actions — all with the element of surprise — and then retreat once again to jungle cover. The important thing, of course, was to avoid any large-scale battle that would give the Americans a chance to mass troops or to bring into play their murderous firepower.

Aguinaldo also saw that in such guerrilla tactics, supply and shelter would be no problem. The rebels could live off the land, aided by sympathetic villagers — among whom they could easily disappear when searched for. By discarding their uniforms, and by hiding their rifles, ammunition, and bolos, the rebels could be quickly transformed into innocent-looking civilians. American soldiers passing through a village would be greeted by shouts of "Amigo!" from the doors of the small huts, but once the Americans were out of sight, the "villagers" would immediately become *Insurrectos* again. The rebels would also enjoy an immense advantage in being accustomed to the Philippine climate. The heat, rain, mud, bad sanitation, and frequently poor food that plagued the Americans had little effect on the rebels.

Beginning in the fall of 1899, the guerrilla war brought bloody discord to the Philippines — savage attacks provoked brutal reprisals, leading inevitably to the spread of unnecessary killing and maiming on both sides. One technique (borrowed from the Spanish) that the Americans used to extract information from rebel prisoners — the "water torture" — was loudly condemned by many people. A prisoner who refused to talk was lowered to the ground, a hose was forced into his mouth, and water was poured slowly over his face and into his stomach. If he continued to remain silent, his stomach would swell painfully as it filled and breathing would become extremely difficult. If not stopped in time the water torture could even kill its victims.

Such practices were, of course, barbaric, yet as its practitioners pointed out, they were not fighting a conventional war; the technique almost always worked, gaining information that often

A group of captured Filipino insurgents.

A company of American infantry drives insurgents through the jungle.

saved the lives of American soldiers. And to the man in the field, this water torture seemed no worse than the rebels' ugly habit of hacking away at wounded soldiers with their wicked bolos.

Whatever the justification for such brutality, or lack of it, Aguinaldo's guerrilla campaign soon managed to produce the hoped-for split in American public opinion. It was widely charged that America had thrown away the high ideals of justice and mercy upon which the nation had been founded. The Anti-Imperialist League, especially, with this new ammunition, became furious in its denunciations of President McKinley and the government. There were angry attempts to send antiwar literature directly to the soldiers in the field, and there were even American calls for defeat of the United States at the hands of the enemy.

The Civil Government
Is Established

While the guerrilla war occupied the attention of press and public
— and even today is the best-remembered aspect of United States-
Philippine involvement — in reality it was less important than the
fact that a new chapter had begun in the civil government of the
islands. With most of the large towns, including Manila, under
American control, and with the greater part of Luzon and Mindinao pacified, life was beginning to return to normal. At this
juncture, in May 1900, a civil commission under the leadership
of William Howard Taft arrived to replace the military government that had ruled for the previous year and a half.

This commission, composed of five Americans and three
Filipinos loyal to the United States, promptly began a sweeping
reorganization that was to earn further respect and loyalty. The
native courts, prison administration, and the police department
were modernized; a new currency system was instituted, and a
large program of public works — particularly for building badly
needed roads — was begun. Perhaps most important of all, agri-
cultural reforms were started, with the intention of transferring
huge tracts of land from the church's control to the hands of small
farmers — a program that bore fruit in a surprisingly short time.
Arrangements were also made for the establishment of a Filipino
legislature, as well as for the extension of many of the guarantees
of the United States Constitution to every Philippine citizen.

One chief reason for the success of this program lay in the
character and personality of Taft himself. Forty-two years old
and a judge of the federal circuit court at the time he was selected
to head the commission, Taft brought to the islands a sympathy
and an understanding that was to set the tone of future American

William Howard Taft (seated, right) with other members of the Philippine Commission. Popular with the Filipinos, Taft often referred to them as "my little brown brothers."

supervision. Against the strong opposition of his military advisors — who felt martial law was needed to offset the activities of Aguinaldo's guerrillas — he decreed that the civil law was supreme. He promised that it would be responsive to every individual and would be benevolent in action.

Taft abolished the color line at social functions, a practice that the Spanish had scrupulously maintained. He made it a point to mix with the native population at meetings, parties, the theater, and even cockfights. He familiarized himself with the geography and nature of the land itself, frequently making trips away from Manila, even occasionally touring the more remote hinterlands. A warm-hearted man with an infectious laugh, he formed the habit of referring to Filipinos as "my little brown brothers." Patronizing as this may sound today, the Filipinos did not resent it, for in Taft's case at least, the phrase seemed more than fitting — he stood well over 6 feet and weighed about 300 pounds.

Unfortunately, while Taft's administration was winning over a large percentage of the population, it made little impression on Aguinaldo's group. The Philippine's best hope for the future, Aguinaldo continued to insist, lay in total independence. So the guerrilla war continued throughout the year 1900, becoming ever more savage and relentless. Even when Aguinaldo's hope for a change in American presidents was dashed — McKinley won easily over Bryan — he did not falter in his now fanatic belief that independence was still possible.

He had already proved that in guerrilla war his untrained and ill-equipped troops could keep the islands in a state of apprehension. Perhaps — who could tell? — the Americans would eventually tire of a war they could not win outright, especially if public opinion in the United States could be brought to the point of disgust.

While these calculations were well founded, they had one

flaw. In order to work, the leadership of Aguinaldo himself was essential. Without his rare abilities, and the powerful appeal of his legend, the entire movement might founder. This fact was well-known to the Americans, of course, yet there was little that could be done about it. The location of Aguinaldo's jungle headquarters was always a closely guarded secret, and it was constantly being shifted. If by some chance the Americans received word of his whereabouts, his spies quickly informed him of his danger and Aguinaldo and his men simply faded like ghosts into the friendly forests.

If it had not been for the daring of one unheralded American army officer, General Frederick Funston, Aguinaldo might have roamed free for years. It was Funston — a thirty-six-year-old colonel in the regular army, but holding the temporary rank of general of volunteers in the Philippines — who conceived and personally led the mission that finally brought about the capture of Aguinaldo.

General Funston
Goes After Aguinaldo

Funston's brilliant plan was hatched with the capture, in February 1901, of a small band of rebels near Funston's headquarters. They were found to be carrying a number of coded dispatches, signed with the name "Colon Magdalo." From previous intelligence work, Funston knew that this referred to Aguinaldo himself. Working feverishly through the night with his intelligence officers, Funston finally was able to break the code.

One of the messages was directed to the rebel command in central Luzon. It contained orders appointing some new officers, and it directed that a picked force of men be sent immediately to Aguinaldo's headquarters. The location of the headquarters was not mentioned, but the message said that the bearer knew the way. The bearer was a man named Segismondo, who had decided soon after capture to switch his allegiance to the Americans, and who had willingly taken the loyalty oath. Aguinaldo, he revealed, was in the village of Palanan, on the northern coast of Luzon. With the leader, he said, were only some fifty men.

Funston knew that it would be useless to send troops directly and openly against Palanan. Aguinaldo would have disappeared long before they arrived, and in any case Funston wanted to take the wily commander alive — a dead Aguinaldo might only provide a martyr for the rebel cause.

Finally, Funston formulated his bold scheme: he would take a picked band of men from among the faithful Filipinos (from the Maccabebees, a tribe that had fostered a long-time hatred for

General Frederick ("Fighting Fred") Funston, author and leader of the brilliant plan to capture Aguinaldo.

[52]

Aguinaldo and that had gladly accepted American intervention from the first), dress them as *Insurrectos,* and send them to Aguinaldo as the requested reinforcements. Funston himself, with three or four other American officers, would accompany the "Little Macs," as they were called, posing as prisoners of war. To play the role of rebel officers, Funston chose two loyal and experienced Filipinos, Lazaro Segovia and Hilario Placido.

With this disguised expedition it would be possible to penetrate directly into Palanan. Once there, Funston and his men would gain access to Aguinaldo's headquarters, overpower the leader, and carry him away. Since Palanan was near the coast, the escape with their captive could easily be managed by having a gunboat waiting offshore at a specified time. If all went well they could skirt the shore on their return journey south and sail right into Manila harbor with their prize.

It was a fantastic and dangerous plan, involving a thousand chances for error and detection, which could easily mean death for all. But General MacArthur, to whom the idea was presented for approval, agreed that it was worth the risk. If Aguinaldo could be caught, the war might be ended, or at least shortened considerably, and many lives would be saved on both sides.

At this point Funston conceived the one element needed to make the operation perfect, though it also increased the dangers of detection. He would send a forged reply to Aguinaldo's message, telling him that the requested men were on the way, bringing with them some American prisoners taken in a small battle en route. If the ruse worked, Funston's band would have an unobstructed route straight into the heart of Palanan. What made this reply possible was the fact that Funston had earlier captured some rebel stationery in a raid. It bore the heading "Brigada Lacuna," which identified it as coming from one of Aguinaldo's most trusted lieutenants. The forged letter would, of course, be written in the same

code Aguinaldo had used, and would carry the forged signature of an appropriate rebel officer. It would be sent from some point along the route of march.

At sundown on March 6, 1901, Funston and four American officers, all dressed as privates, together with eighty Little Macs, boarded the gunboat that would take them part of the way up the Luzon coast. General MacArthur was on the dock to see the party off. Taking Funston's hand he said in a voice full of concern: "This is a desperate undertaking. I fear that I shall never see you again."

In the darkness the gunboat steamed far out to sea to avoid any possibility of detection, then headed north. Four days later it bore in toward shore but halted half a mile out. The party was to use several large canoes for landing, and it was here that Funston met his first setback. The rough seas swamped each boat as it was lowered. They could be righted but the risk of using them, Funston saw, was too great. He made an instant decision: the gunboat would have to run right into the beach and risk being spotted. Fortunately, this was accomplished without incident, the eighty-five men were disembarked, and the boat steamed away well before dawn.

The boat was under orders to return, farther north, on March 25. Funston had fifteen days to penetrate the jungle, reach Palanan, capture Aguinaldo, and lead his party to the rendezvous.

To reach the first point of contact, the village of Casiguran, Funston took his men along the shoreline. This, he thought, would be easier going than trying to hack a direct path through the jungle. He soon found that he was mistaken, for the men were frequently forced to wade waist-deep around the mangrove thickets at the water's edge. This left them soaked and miserable from the salty ocean water as well as drenched in sweat due to the boiling sun.

The expedition's movement was slow and it required two days

to reach Casiguran. Here the first test was passed: the villagers greeted them as true rebels, and proceeded to insult and revile the American "prisoners." They listened with admiration to the tales the Little Macs told of the "battle" in which the Americans had been captured. Village musicians even turned out to offer the heroes a serenade. There was one anxious moment when Funston heard a rumor that Aguinaldo had recently added 400 men to his headquarters force. Luckily, this turned out to be untrue. Everything went so well at Casiguran, in fact, that Funston's only worry was that the Macs might get carried away in their boasting and say the wrong thing.

It was from Casiguran that the Mac officers, Segovia and Placido, sent the forged letter to Aguinaldo by a messenger recruited from the village. Then, after resting for two days, the party resumed its journey to Palanan.

Now came the hardest part of the trip, a seven-day march through some of the most rugged terrain in Luzon. The additional food supplies Funston had hoped to pick up at Casiguran had not been available, so provisions were very low and the men were allowed only two very small meals a day, one in the morning and one at night. Many of them made up the deficiency by eating such things as vegetation and snails.

After a week of fording rain-swollen streams, struggling up high cliffs, and slogging through swamps and jungle undergrowth, the party was within a day of Palanan. It was here that they encountered some rebels who were sent out by Aguinaldo to meet them. The leader, who had been completely deceived by the forged letter, was anxious to question the American prisoners.

On the eighth day from Casiguran, Funston and his weary men arrived at the Palanan River. On the opposite bank they could see the village they had risked so much to reach. But here they found themselves faced with a formidable obstacle. Only one

small boat was available for crossing the river; it could hold only seven or eight men. Thus, at least a half-hour would be needed to get the entire party to the other side. This raised a real danger, because during the crossing the party would be split, and nothing could be done until every man was ready for action. Moreover, during that anxious half-hour the Little Macs would have to continue to play their role before the curious Palanan villagers.

Aguinaldo himself greeted the first boatload, which included Segovia and Placido but not Funston, who had to remain behind with the other "prisoners." The two disguised officers were taken by Aguinaldo to his office on the upper floor of his residence. Playing for time, they gave lengthy answers to the questions put to them, and supplied long and enthusiastic accounts of their "battle" with the Americans.

At last all the Little Macs, with their "prisoners," were across the river and lined up in the village square near the rebel guards, about forty in number. In Aguinaldo's office, Segovia casually stepped out to the balcony, saw that everything was in readiness, then signaled with a wave of his hat. At once the quiet of the village was torn by a volley from the rifles of the Macs. A number of rebel guards went down, and the rest, stunned and confused, scattered into the jungle.

In his office, Aguinaldo heard the firing and thought it had come from his own men as a salute to the new arrivals. He went to the window to order silence. The next instant he was seized by the strong arms of Placido and pinned to the floor, where he would be relatively safe from stray bullets. The five rebel officers in the room instantly reached for their own arms, but Segovia's pistol was suddenly blazing away at them. Two fell wounded; the others dashed from the room. Seconds later, Funston burst in and informed the incredulous Aguinaldo that he was a prisoner of the American army.

[57]

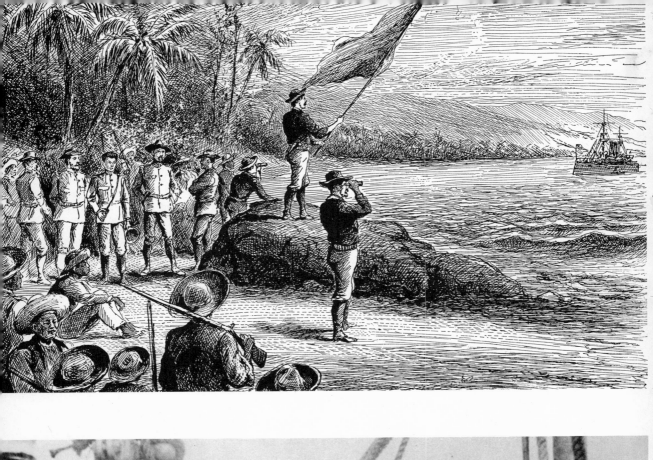

The journey to the rendezvous with the gunboat on the shore of Palanan Bay, while extremely hazardous, required only a few hours and was accomplished without mishap. On the evening of March 25, the raiders and their prisoner were safely at sea.

Funston and his men went ashore at Manila to a hero's welcome. News of the mission's fantastic success reached the American public a few days later and was blazoned on front pages all over the country. For their spectacular feat, every member of the raiding party was rewarded. Funston himself was later, by direction of President McKinley, appointed to the permanent rank of brigadier general in the regular United States Army.

Above: Funston signals the capture of Aguinaldo to the gunboat offshore. Below: rare photograph shows the captured Emilio Aguinaldo boarding the gunboat Vicksburg.

[59]

The Insurrection
Winds Down

With the capture of the rebel leader, the end of the Philippine Insurrection was in sight. Aguinaldo, feeling that his leaderless followers would steadily disintegrate into smaller and less effective units if they kept on fighting, and deciding that further bloodshed was useless in any case, willingly took the oath of allegiance to the United States at Manila on April 19, 1901. Then he called on all the *Insurrectos* to lay down their arms.

This, however, did not bring an immediate end to the guerrilla campaign, for many die-hard rebels continued to hold out. Especially in the southern portion of the country, on the island of Samar where the Moros considered themselves almost a separate nation, did the blood-spilling go on. Now and then it even rose to new heights of ferocity. But these outbreaks were localized and did not seriously affect the general peace that now descended on the Philippines.

In September 1901, President McKinley was felled by an assassin's bullet, and his vice-president, Theodore Roosevelt, took the reins of office. Roosevelt encouraged Taft, who was a personal friend, in his liberal governing policies, and by the summer of 1902 nearly all fighting had ceased. At last, three years after its beginnings, President Roosevelt declared an end to the Insurrection. A full pardon was granted to all those rebels who had fought against the United States, including Emilio Aguinaldo.

Theodore Roosevelt in a photograph taken in 1901 when he succeeded the assassinated McKinley as president.

The Road to Independence

If the American role in the Philippines was questionable at first, at least the part it played during succeeding decades deserves praise. Less than five years after termination of the fighting, Filipinos were given the right to elect their own assembly, and later, under President Woodrow Wilson, a Bill of Rights was framed. Among other things, this extended the voting privilege to all males who were twenty-one years old and widened the powers of the legislature. More important, it made a definite promise of independence. Then, in 1934 the Philippines were granted a commonwealth status, allowing nearly total self-government under American supervision. At this same time a specific date for independence was set — 1946, appropriately on July 4.

Throughout World War II, when the Philippines became a fiercely ravaged battleground, with American and Filipino fighting side by side to throw back the Japanese invaders, that date was constantly in sight. When the war ended, the people of the Philippines were very much aware that independence was only a little more than a year away.

On July 4, 1946, in Washington, D.C., President Harry S. Truman issued a proclamation. It recounted the history of the relationship of the Philippines and America, the stages in the development of the new country, praised "the glorious part taken by the Filipino people in the recent terrible war," and ended: "On behalf of the United States of America, I do hereby recognize the independence of the Philippines as a separate and self-governing nation."

Emilio Aguinaldo as he appeared in later years.

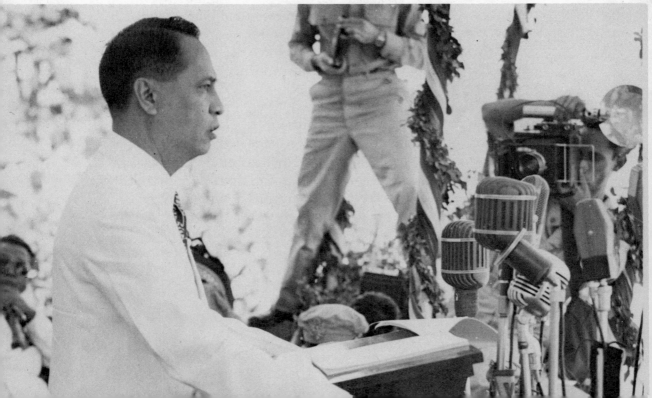

In Manila that day, great celebrations began, some of which were to last for a week. At the official residence of the first president, Manuel Roxas y Acuña, a gala reception was held. In attendance, among hundreds of other guests from many countries, was General Douglas MacArthur, famous son of the officer who had played a principle part in crushing the Insurrection. Also present in a post of honor, his dark eyes still alert and undimmed, was the seventy-eight-year-old Emilio Aguinaldo.

Above: General Douglas MacArthur delivering an address in July 1946, at ceremonies in Manila marking the end of U.S. sovereignty and the beginning of Philippine independence. Below: first President of the new Philippine Republic, Manuel Roxas, delivers his inaugural address in Manila.

Bibliography and Further Reading

Agoncillo, T. *Malolos: The Crisis of the Republic*. Manila: University of the Philippines, 1960.

Aguinaldo, E. *True Version of the Philippine Revolution*. Tarlac, 1899.

Freeman, N. *A Soldier in the Philippines*. 1901.

Funston, F. *Memories of Two Wars: Cuba and the Philippines*. 1914.

Kennedy, C. *The Capture of Aguinaldo*. 1902.

Leckie, R. *The Wars of America*. New York: Harper and Row, 1968.

Porter, D., *Sailing the Sulu Sea*. 1940.

Sexton, W. *Soldiers in the Sun: An Adventure in Imperialism*. (Reprint of 1939 edition) Freeport: Books for Libraries.

Wilcox, M. *Harper's History of the War in the Philippines*. 1900.

Wolff, L. *America's Forgotten Bid for Empire*. Boston: Little Brown, 1961.

Zaide, G. *The Philippine Revolution*. New York, 1954.

Zornow, W. "Funston Captures Aguinaldo." *American Heritage*. February 1958.

Index

United States Navy. *See* Navy, United States
United States policy toward Philippines, 43, 48, 50
United States Senate, 32, 33, 37
United States soldiers, 29, 30

Vietnam, 9
Villages, Philippine. *See* Philippine Islands
Visayan, language, 9

Volunteers, American Philippine Insurrection, 51
Von Diederichs, Admiral, 19
Voting privilege to Filipinos, 63

Wake Island, 27
Washington, D.C., 33
Water torture, 44, 47
Wilson, Woodrow, 63
World War II, 63

About the Author

John E. Walsh has written two other books in the Focus series: *The Sinking of the USS Maine*, and *The Mayflower Compact*. Among his other writings are scholarly biographies of poets Emily Dickinson and Francis Thompson. In 1969 his *Poe the Detective* was picked as best fact-crime book of the year by the Mystery Writers of America. A writer of sports as well, he takes special pride in an article in which he proved the old legend that Babe Ruth in the 1932 World Series predicted his own home run. An editor by profession, Mr. Walsh currently has a number of projects under way, mong them a newly researched account of the Wright Brothers. With his wife and four children, he lives in New Jersey.